Hippocrene

CHILDREN'S ILLUSTRATED ARABIC DICTIONARY

ENGLISH - ARABIC
ARABIC - ENGLISH

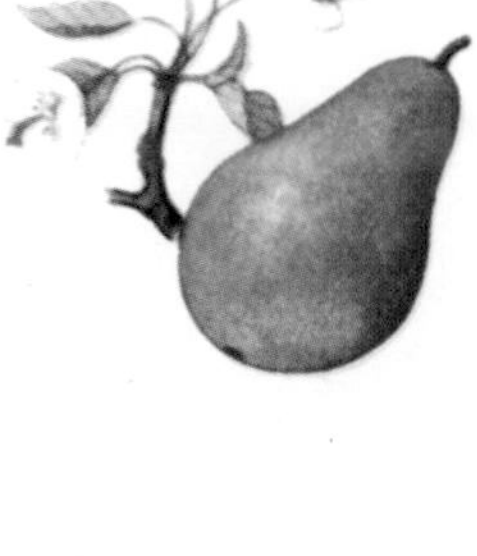

Compiled and translated by the Editors of Hippocrene Books

Interior illustrations by S. Grant (24, 81, 88); J. Gress (page 10, 21, 24, 37, 46, 54, 59, 65, 72, 75, 77); K. Migliorelli (page 13, 14, 18, 19, 20, 21, 22, 25, 31, 32, 37, 39, 40, 46, 47, 66, 71, 75, 76, 82, 86, 87); B. Swidzinska (page 9, 11, 12, 13, 14, 16, 23, 27, 28, 30, 32, 33, 35, 37, 38, 41, 42, 45, 46, 47, 48, 49, 50, 52, 53, 56, 57, 58, 59, 60, 61, 62, 63, 66, 68, 69, 70, 71, 72, 73, 75, 77, 78, 79, 83), N. Zhukov (page 8, 13, 14, 17, 18, 23, 27, 29, 33, 34, 39, 40, 41, 52, 64, 65, 71, 72, 73, 78, 84, 86, 88).

Design, prepress, and production: Graafiset International Inc.

Hippocrene Children's Illustrated Arabic Dictionary

Fourth printing, paperback edition, 2008

Cataloging-in-Publication Data available from the Library of Congress.

ISBN-13: 978-0-7818-0891-0
ISBN-10: 0-7818-0891-X

Printed in China.

For information, address:
Hippocrene Books, Inc.
171 Madison Avenue
New York, NY 10016
www.hippocrenebooks.com

INTRODUCTION

With their absorbent minds, infinite curiosities and excellent memories, children have enormous capacities to master many languages. All they need is exposure and encouragement.

The easiest way to learn a foreign language is to simulate the same natural method by which a child learns English. The natural technique is built on the concept that language is representational of concrete objects and ideas. The use of pictures and words are the natural way for children to begin to acquire a new language.

The concept of this Illustrated Dictionary is to allow children to build vocabulary and initial competency naturally. Looking at the pictorial content of the Dictionary and saying and matching the words in connection to the drawings gives children the opportunity to discover the foreign language and thus, a new way to communicate.

The drawings in the Dictionary are designed to capture children's imaginations and make the learning process interesting and entertaining, as children return to a word and picture repeatedly until they begin to recognize it.

The beautiful images and clear presentation make this dictionary a wonderful tool for unlocking your child's multilingual potential.

Deborah Dumont, M.A., M.Ed.,
Child Psychologist and Educational Consultant

Arabic Pronunciation

Letter		*Pronunciation system used*
ا	alif	**aa** like in English 'had' when used as a vowel
ب	baa	**b** as in English 'bent'
ت	taa	**t** as in English 'today'
ث	thaa	**th** like the *th* in English 'think'
ج	jiim	**j** as in English 'just'
ح	Haa	**H** an emphatic *h* pronounced with a strong expulsion of air from the chest
خ	khaa	**kh** like the guttural *ch* in the Scottish pronunciation of 'loch' but more from the throat
د	daal	**d** as in English 'day'
ذ	dhaal	**dh** like the *th* in English 'this'
ر	raa	**r** a rolled *r*
ز	zain	**z** like the *z* in English 'zebra'
س	siin	**s** like the hissing *s* in English 'beside'
ش	shiin	**sh** as in English 'ship'
ص	Saad	**S** an emphatic *s* formed by placing the tongue against the lower palate instead of against the teeth
ض	Daad	**D** an emphatic *d* formed by placing the tongue against the lower palate instead of against the teeth
ط	Taa	**T** an emphatic *t* formed by placing the tongue against the lower palate instead of against the teeth
ظ	Zaa	**Z** an emphatic *z* formed by placing the tongue against the lower palate instead of against the teeth
ع	Ain	**'** a very strong guttural sound produced by compression of the throat and expulsion of the breath

Letter		Pronunciation system used
غ	Ghain	**gh** an exaggerated gargling, uvular r-sound formed by pressing the tongue against the lower palate
ف	faa	**f** as in English ‘fire’
ق	qaaf	**q** a k-sound produced in the throat somewhat behind the *c* in English ‘cool’
ك	kaaf	**k** as in English ‘key’
ل	laam	**l** as in English ‘land’
م	miim	**m** as in English ‘man’
ن	nuun	**n** as in English ‘no’
هـ	haa	**h** as in English ‘hand’
و	waw	**w** as in English ‘wet’ when used as a consonant **oo** as in English ‘boot’ when used as a vowel
ي	yaa	**y** as in English ‘yesterday’ when used as a consonant **ee** as in English ‘see’ when used as a vowel
ة	taa marbooTa	**a** feminine ending of nouns or adjectives
ـَ	fatHa	vowel sign indicating a short *a* like in English ‘man’
ـِ	kasra	vowel sign indicating *i* like in English ‘ring’
ـُ	Damma	vowel sign indicating a short *u* like in English ‘book’
ـْ	sukoon	sign written above a consonant indicating a consonant cluster
ـّ	shadda	sign indicating the doubling of a consonant
ء	hamza	**’** a click pronounced by a quick compression of the upper part of the throat
ـٌ ـٍ ـً	tanween	**un/in/an** three signs used to define the end of nouns and adjectives

airplane طائِرَة

Taa-'ira

alligator قاطُور

qaa-Toor

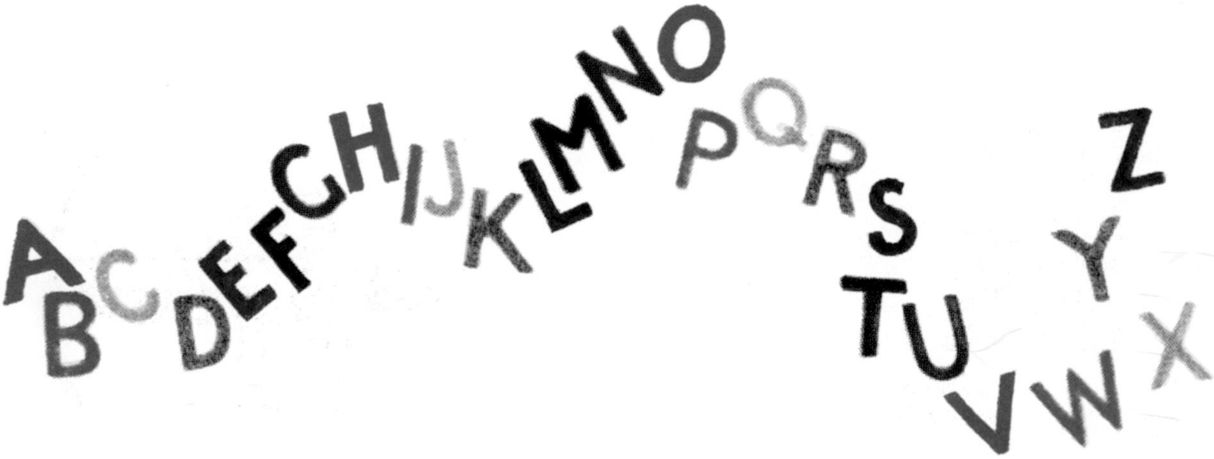

alphabet أبْجَدِيَّة

ab-ja-diy-ya

antelope ظَبي

Za-bee

antlers قَرنُ الوَعِل

qar-nul wa-eel

apple تُفَّاحَة

tuf-faa-Ha

aquarium حَوْضُ الأَسْمَاك

Haw-Dul as-maak

arch قَنْطَرَة

qan-Ta-ra

arrow سَهْم

sahm

autumn خَرِيف

kha-reef

baby طِفْلٌ رَضِيع

Tif-lun ra-Dee'

backpack شَنْطَةُ ظَهْر

shan-Ta-tu Zahr

badger غُرَيْر

ghu-rair

baker خَبَّاز

khab-baaz

ball كُرَة

ku-ra

balloon بالُون

baa-lon

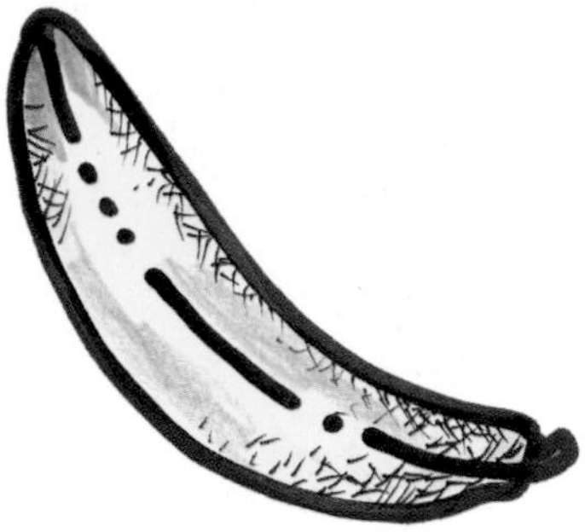

banana مَوْزَة

maw-za

barley شَعِير

sha'-eer

barrel بِرْمِيل

bir-meel

basket سَلَّة

sal-la

bat خُفَّاش

khuf-faash

beach شاطِىء

shaa-Ti'

bear دُبّ

dubb

beaver قُنْدُس

qun-dus

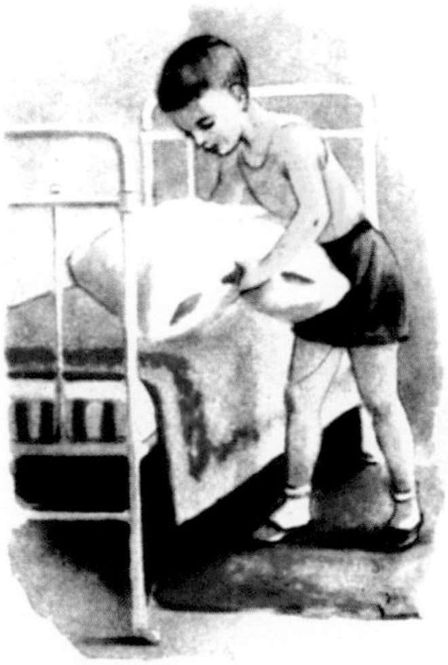

bed سَرِير

sa-reer

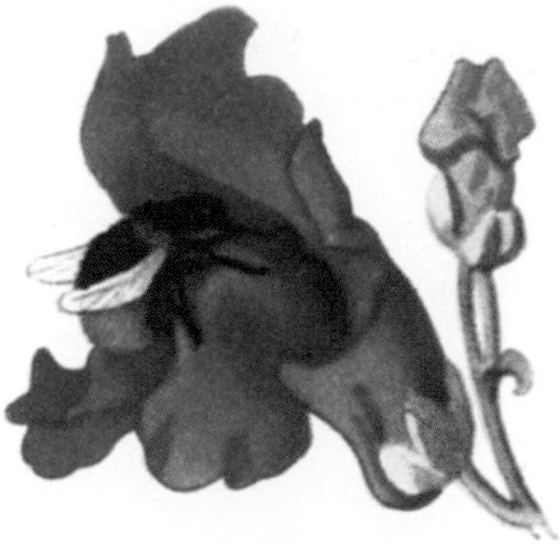

bee نَحْلَة

naH-la

beetle خُنْفُساء

khun-fu-saa'

bell جَرَس

ja-ras

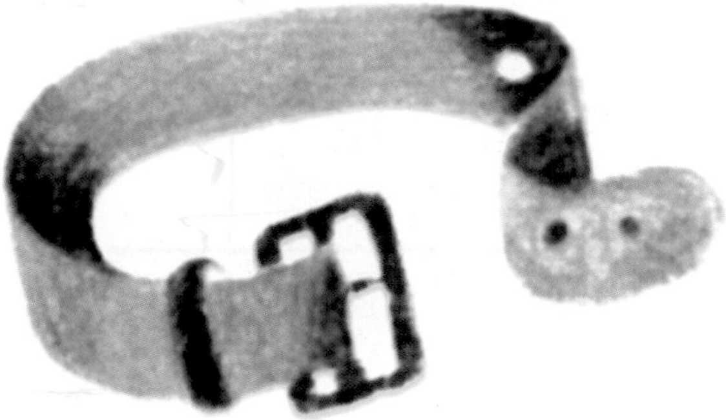

belt حِزَام

Hi-zaam

bench بَنْك

bank

bicycle دَرَّاجَة

dar-raa-ja

binoculars مِنْظار

min-Zaar

bird طَيْر

Tair

birdcage قَفَص

qa-faS

black أَسْوَد

as-wad

blocks قَوَالِبُ البِنَاء

qa-waa-li-bul bi-naa'

blossom نَوْر

nawr

blue أَزْرَق

az-rak

boat قَارِب

qaa-rib

bone عَظْم

'aZm

book كِتَاب

ki-taab

boot حِذَاء عَالي السَاق

Hi-dhaa' 'aa-leel saaq

bottle زُجَاجَة

zu-jaa-ja

bowl سُلْطانِيَّة

sul-Taa-niy-ya

boy وَلَد

wa-lad

bracelet سِوَار

si-waar

branch غُصْن

ghuSn

bread خُبْز

khubz

breakfast فَطُور

fa-Toor

bridge جِسْر

jisr

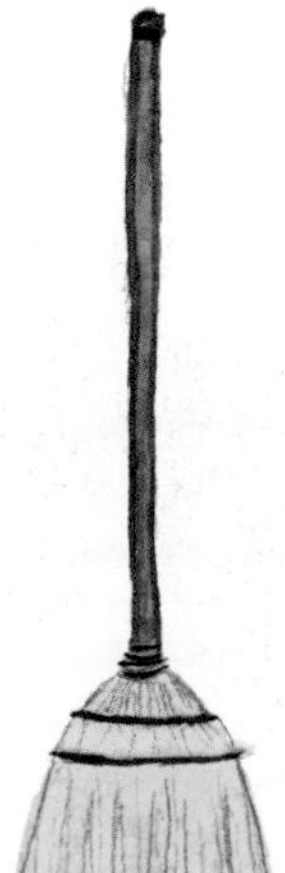

broom مِكْنَسَة

mik-na-sa

brother أَخ

akh

brown أَسْمَر

as-mar

brush فُرْشَاة

fur-shaat

bucket دَلْو

dalu

bulletin board لَوْحَةُ الإِعْلانَات

law-Ha-tul i'-laa-naat

bumblebee نَحْلَةٌ كَبِيرَة طَنَّانَة

naH-la-tun ka-bee-ra Tan-naa-na

butterfly فَرَاشَة

fa-raa-sha

cab تَاكْسِي

taak-see

cabbage كُرُنْب/مَلْفُوف

ku-runb/mal-foof

cactus صُبَّيْر

Sub-bayr

café مَقْهَى

maq-ha

cake تُورْتَة/كَعْكَة

toor-ta/ka'-ka

camel جَمَل

ja-mal

camera كامِيرَا

kaa-mee-ra

candle شَمْعَة

sham-‘a

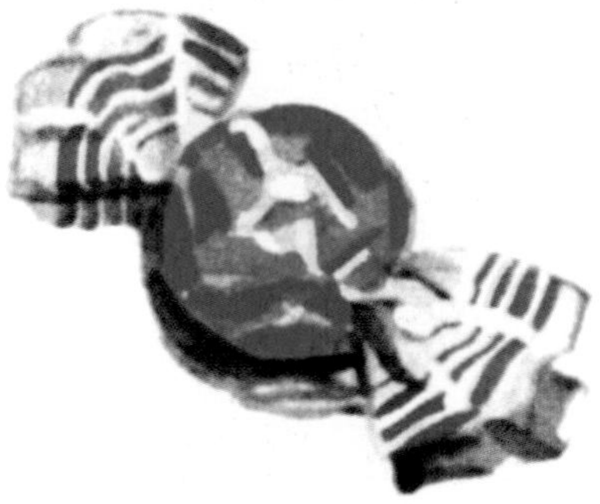

candy بُونْبُون/مُلَبَّس

boon-boon/mu-lab-bas

canoe قَارِبُ هِنْدِيّ

qaa-ri-bun hin-diy

cap طَاقِيَّة

Taa-qiy-ya

captain قُبْطان

qub-Taan

car سَيَّارَة

say-yaa-ra

card وَرَقُ اللَعِب

wa-ra-qul la-'ib

carpet سَجَّادَة

saj-jaa-da

carrot جَزَرَة

ja-za-ra

(to) carry حَمَلَ

Ha-ma-la

castle قَصْر

qaSr

cat قِطَّة
qiT-Ta

cave كَهْف
kahf

chair كُرْسِيّ
kur-siy

cheese جُبْن
jubn

cherry كَرَز
ka-raz

chimney مَدْخَنَة
mad-kha-na

chocolate شُوكُولاتَه

shoo-koo-laa-ta

Christmas tree شَجَرَةُ عِيدِ المِيْلاد

sha-ja-ra-tu ‘eedil mee-laad

circus سِيرْك

seerk

(to) climb تَسَلَّقَ

ta-sal-la-qa

cloud سَحَاب

sa-Haab

clown مُهَرِّج

mu-har-rij

coach عَرَبَة

'a-ra-ba

coat مِعْطَف

mi'-Taf

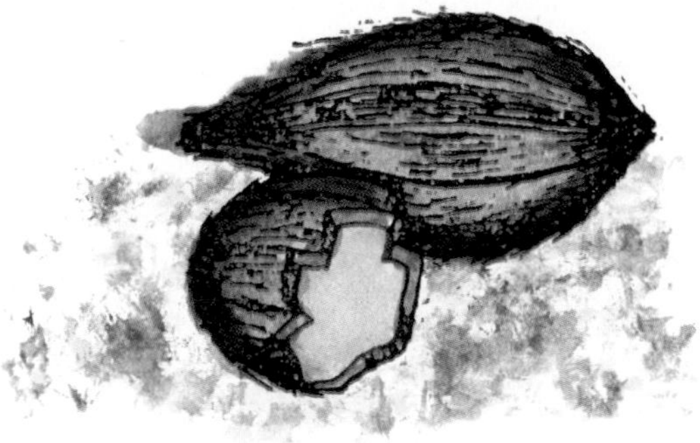

coconut جَوْزُ الهِنْد

jaw-zul hind

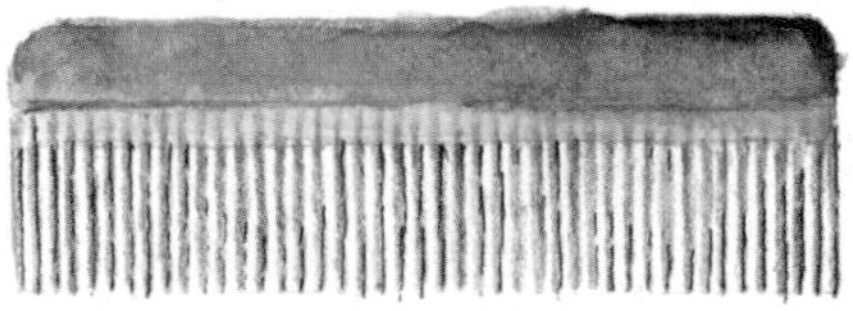

comb مِشْط

mishT

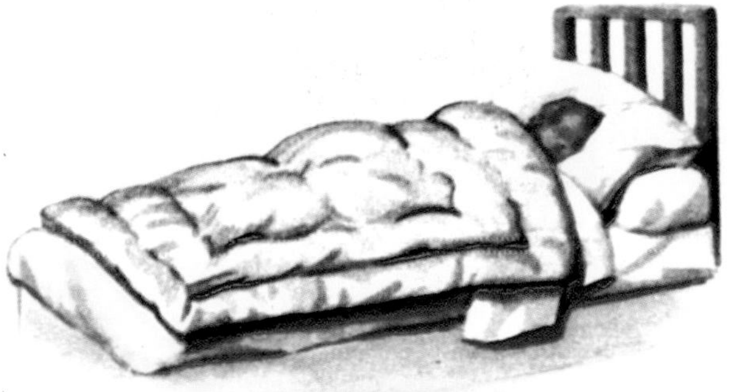

comforter لِحَاف

li-Haaf

compass بُوْصُلَة

baw-Su-la

(to) cook طَبَخَ

Ta-ba-kha

cork فَلِّينَة

fal-lee-na

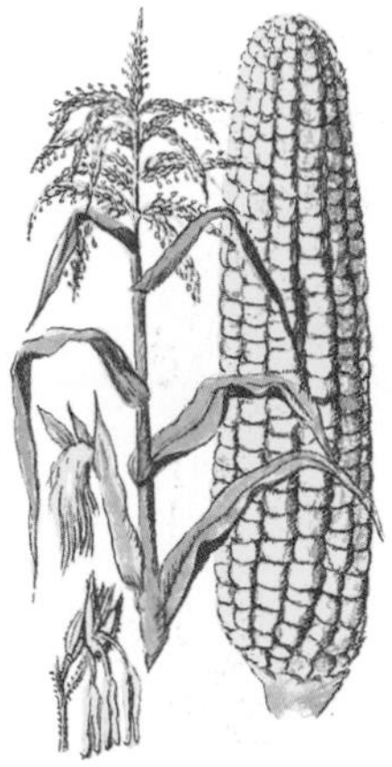

corn ذُرَة

dhu-ra

cow بَقَرَة

ba-qa-ra

cracker بَسْكَوِيت

bas-ka-weet

cradle مَهْد

mahd

(to) crawl زَحَفَ

za-Ha-fa

(to) cross عَبَرَ

'a-ba-ra

crown تاج

taaj

(to) cry بَكَى

ba-ka

cucumber خِيَار

khi-yaar

curtain سِتَارَة

si-taa-ra

(to) dance رَقَصَ

ra-qa-Sa

dandelion طَرَخْشَقُون

Ta-rakh-sha-qoon

date تارِيخ

taa-reekh

deer أَيِّل

ay-yil

desert صَحْراء

SaH-raa'

desk مَكْتَب

mak-tab

dirty قَذِر

qa-dhir

dog كَلْب

kalb

doghouse كُشْكُ الكَلْب

kush-kul kalb

doll عَرُوسَة

'a-roo-sa

dollhouse بَيْتُ العَرُوسَة

bayt-tul 'a-roo-sa

dolphin دُلْفِين

dol-feen

donkey حِمَار

Hi-maar

dragon تِنِّين

tin-neen

dragonfly سُرْمان

sur-maan

(to) draw رَسَمَ

ra-sa-ma

dress فُسْتان

fus-taan

(to) drink شَرِبَ

sha-ri-ba

drum طَبْل

Tabl

duck بَطّ

baTT

eagle نَسْر

nasr

(to) eat أَكَلَ

a-ka-la

egg بَيْض

baiD

eggplant باذِنْجان

baa-dhin-jaan

eight ثَمَانِيَة

tha-maa-ni-ya

elbow كُوْع

koo'

elephant فِيْل

feel

empty فارِغ

faa-righ

engine قاطِرَة

qaa-Ti-ra

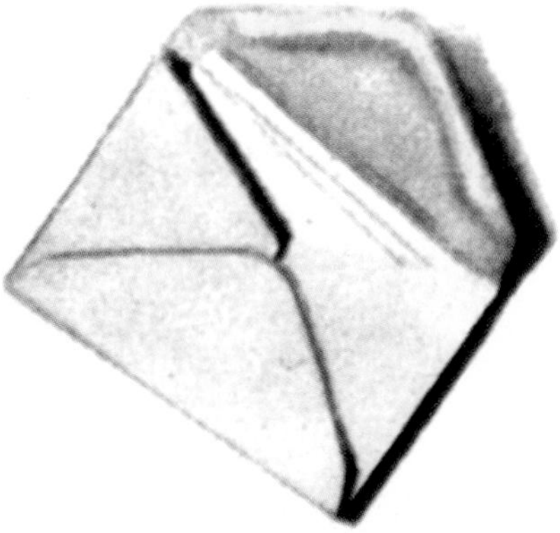

envelope ظَرْف

Zarf

escalator سُلَّمٌ مُتَحَرِّك

sul-la-mun mu-ta-Har-rik

Eskimo أسْكيمو

as-ki-mo

(to) explore اِسْتَكْشَفَ

is-tak-sha-fa

eye عَيْن

'ain

face وَجْه

wajh

fan مِرْوَحَة

mir-wa-Ha

father أَب

ab

fear خَوْف

khawf

feather رِيشَة

ree-sha

(to) feed عَلَفَ

'a-la-fa

fence سُور

soor

fern خِنْشار

khin-shaar

field حَقْل

Haql

field mouse فَأْرٌ بَرِّيّ

fa-'run bar-riy

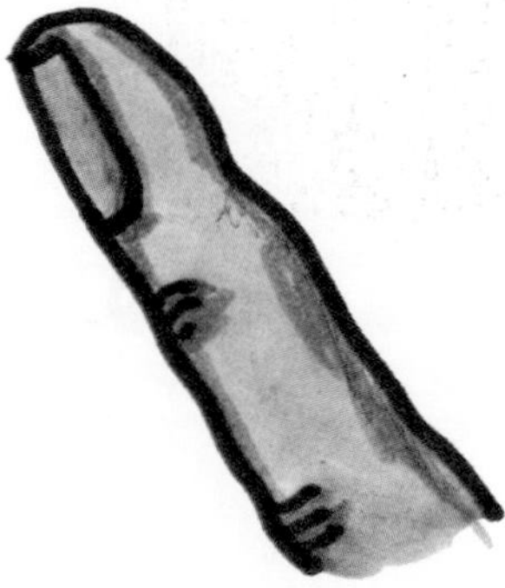

finger إِصْبَع

iS-ba'

fir tree شَجَرَةُ التَنّوب

sha-ja-ra-tul tan-noob

fire نار
naar

fish سَمَكَة
sa-ma-ka

(to) fish اِصْطادَ
is-Taa-da

fist قَبْضَةُ اليَد
qab-Da-tul yad

five خَمْسَة
kham-sa

flag عَلَم
'a-lam

flashlight مِصْباحُ جَيْب

miS-baaHu jayb

(to) float طَفَا

Ta-fa

flower زَهْرَة

zah-ra

(to) fly طارَ

Taa-ra

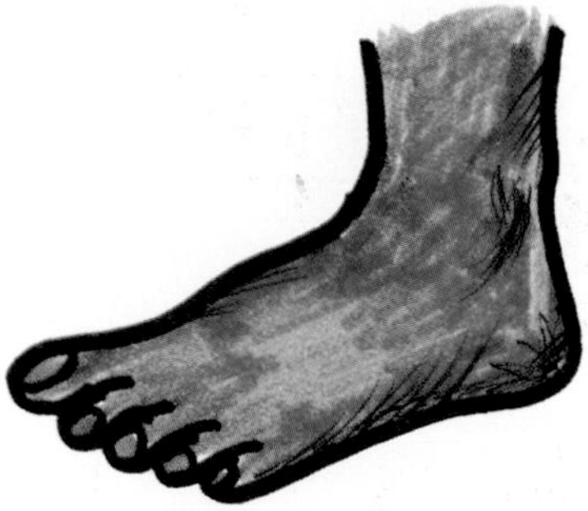

foot قَدَم

qa-dam

fork شَوْكَة

shaw-ka

fountain نافُورَة

naa-foo-ra

four أَرْبَعَة

ar-ba-'a

fox ثَعْلَب

tha'-lab

frame بِرْواز

bir-waaz

friend صَدِيق

Sa-deeq

frog ضِفْدِعَة

Dif-di-'a

fruit فاكِهَة

faa-ki-ha

furniture أَثَاث

a-thaath

garden حَدِيقَة

Ha-dee-qa

gate بَوَّابَة

baw-waa-ba

(to) gather جَمَعَ

ja-ma-'a

geranium غُرْنُوقِيّ

ghur-nu-qiy

giraffe زَرَافَة

za-raa-fa

girl بِنْت

bint

(to) give أَعْطَى *a'-Ta*

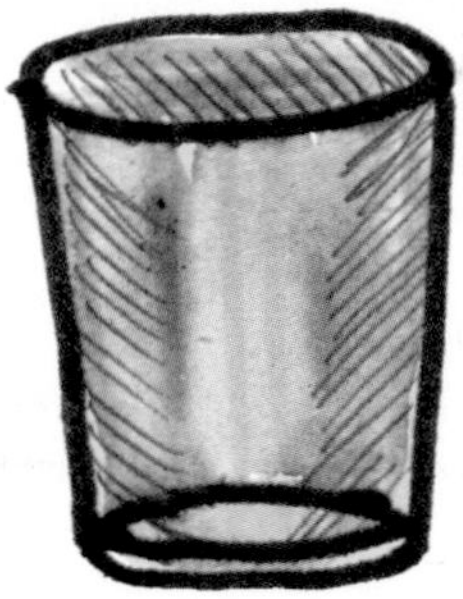

glass كَأْس *ka's*

glasses نَظَّارَة *naZ-Zaa-ra*

globe الكُرَة الأَرْضِيَّة *al-ku-ral ar-Diy-ya*

glove قُفَّاز *quf-faaz*

goat مِعْزَى *mi'-za*

goldfish سَمَكٌ ذَهَبِيّ

sa-makun dha-ha-biy

"Good Night" لَيْلَة سَعِيدَة

lai-la sa'ee-da

"Good-bye" مَعَ السَلامَة

ma'as sa-laa-ma

goose وَزَّة

waz-za

grandfather جَدّ

jadd

grandmother جَدَّة

jad-da

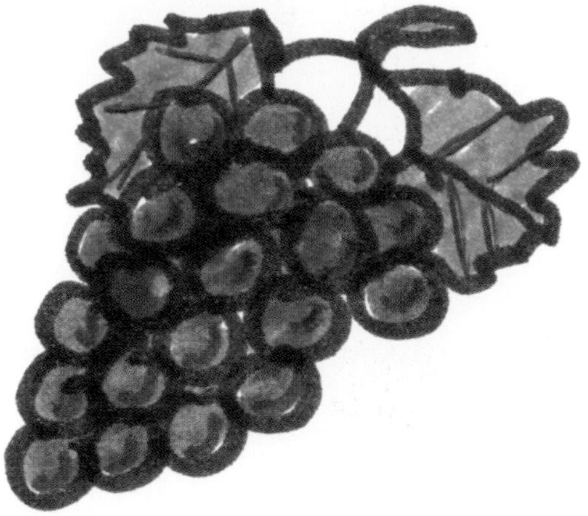

grapes عِنَب

'i-nab

grasshopper جُنْدُب

jun-dub

green أَخْضَر

akh-Dar

greenhouse بَيْتٌ زُجَاجِيّ

bay-tun zu-jaa-jiy

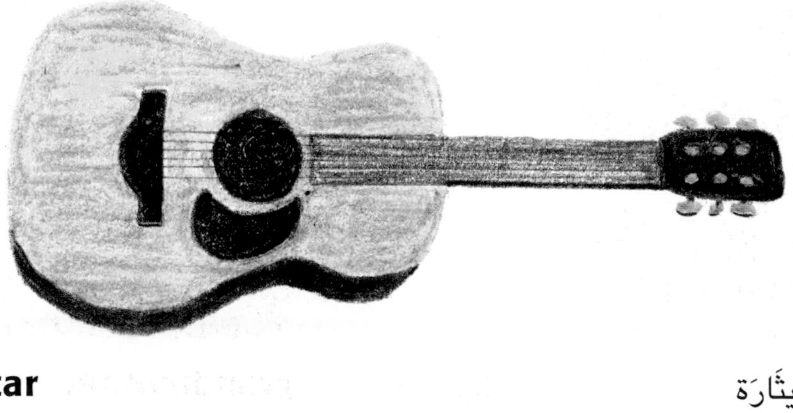

guitar قِيثَارَة

qi-thaa-ra

hammer مِطْرَقة

miT-ra-qa

hammock أُرْجُوحَةٌ شَبَكِيَّة

ur-ju-Ha-tun sha-ba-kiy-ya

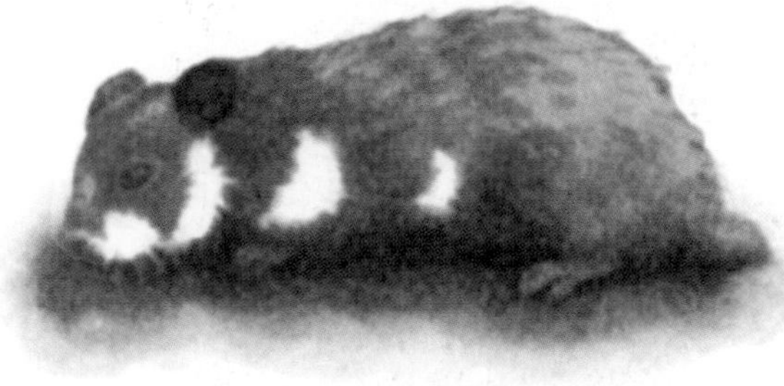

hamster هَمْسْتِر

hams-ter

hand يَد

yad

handbag حَقِيبَةُ يَد

Ha-qi-ba-tu yad

handkerchief مَنْدِيل

mand-deel

harvest حَصْد

HaSd

hat قُبَّعَة

qub-ba-'a

hay تِبْن

tibn

headdress زِيْنَةٌ لِلرأْس

zai-na-tun lil-ra's

heart قَلْب

qalb

hedgehog قُنْفُذ

qun-fudh

hen دَجَاجَة

da-jaa-ja

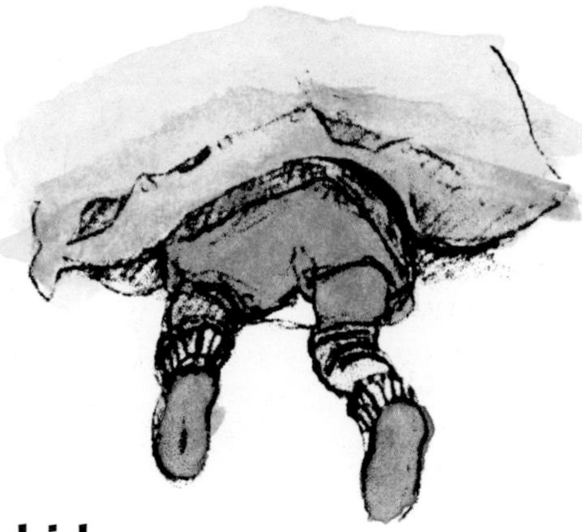

(to) hide اِخْتَبَأَ

ikh-ta-ba'a

highway طَرِيقٌ عام

Ta-ree-qun 'aam

honey عَسَل

'asal

horns قُرُون

qu-roon

horse حِصَان

Hi-Saan

horseshoe حَدْوَة
Had-wa

hourglass ساعَةٌ رَمْلِيَّة
saa-'a-tun ram-liy-ya

house بَيْت
bayt

(to) hug اِحْتَضَنَ
iH-ta-Da-na

hydrant مِضَخَةُ الحَرِيق
mi-Da-kha-tul Ha-reeq

ice cream جِيْلاَتِي/بُوْظَة

ge-laat-ti/boo-Za

ice cubes مُكَعَّبَاتُ ثَلْج

mu-ka'-'a-baa-tu thalj

ice-skating تَزَلُّج عَلَى الجَلِيد

ta-zal-luj 'alal ja-leed

instrument آلَةٌ مُوسِيقِيَّة

aa-la-tun moo-see-qiy-ya

iris سَوْسَن

saw-san

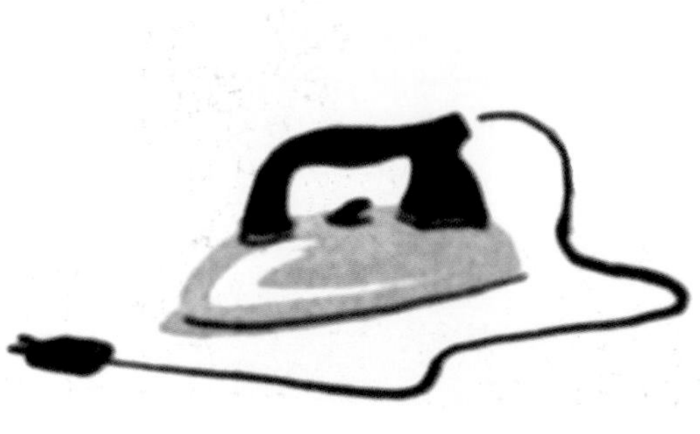

iron مِكْواة

mik-waat

island جَزِيرَة

ja-zee-ra

jacket جاكِيت

jaa-ket

jam مُرَبَّى

mu-rab-ba

jigsaw puzzle أَحْجِيَةُ الصُوَر المَقْطُوعَة

aH-ji-ya-tul Su-war al-maq-Tu'a

jockey جُوكِي

jo-kee

juggler بَهْلَوَان

bah-la-waan

(to) jump قَفَزَ

qa-fa-za

kangaroo كَنْغَر

kan-ghar

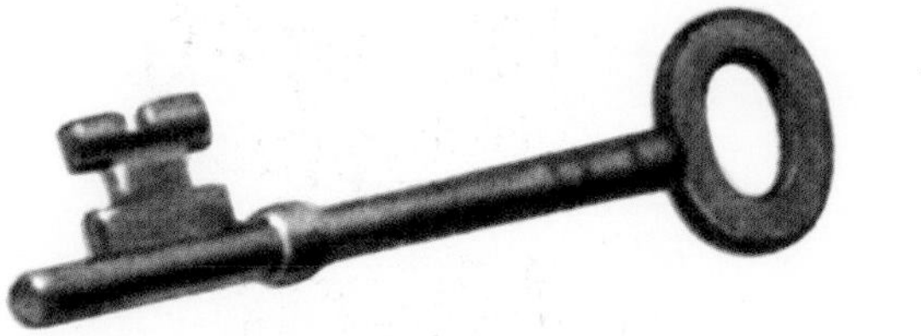

key مِفْتاح

mif-taaH

kitten قُطَيْطَة

qu-Tay-Ta

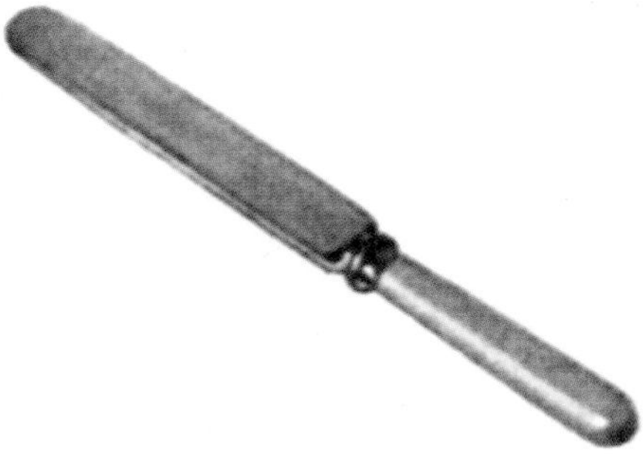

knife سِكِّين

sik-keen

knight فارِس

faa-ris

(to) knit حَبَكَ

Ha-ba-ka

knot عُقْدَة

'uq-da

koala bear الكُوال

al-ko-waal

ladder سُلَّم
sul-lam

ladybug دُعْسُوقَة
du'-su-qa

lamb حَمَل
Ha-mal

lamp مِصْبَاح
mis-baaH

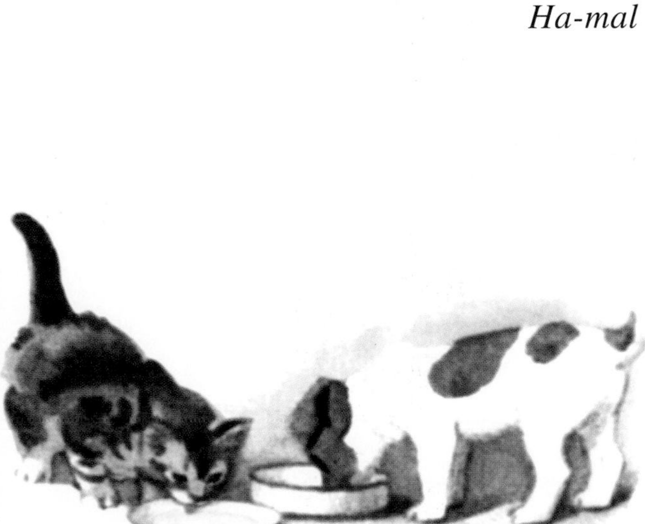

(to) lap لَحَسَ
la-Ha-sa

laughter ضَحِك
Da-Hik

lavender خُزَامَى

khu-zaa-ma

lawn mower مِحَشّ

mi-Hash

leaf وَرَقَة

wa-ra-qa

leg رِجْل

rijl

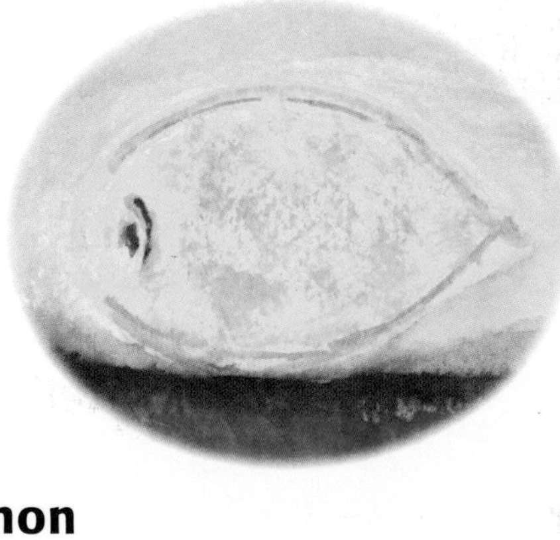

lemon لَيْمُون

lay-moon

lettuce خَسّ

khass

lightbulb لَمْبَةٌ كَهْرَبائِيَّة

lam-ba-tun kah-ra-baa-iy-ya

lighthouse مَنَارَة

ma-naa-ra

lilac لَيْلَك

lay-lak

lion أَسَد

a-sad

(to) listen اِسْتَمَعَ

is-ta-ma-'a

lobster كَرْكَنْد

kar-kand

lock كَالُون

kaa-loon

lovebird البَبَّغَاءُ المُتَيَّمَة

al-bab-ba-ghaa-'ul mu-tay-ya-ma

luggage أَمْتِعَة

am-ti-'a

lumberjack حَطَّاب

HaT-Taab

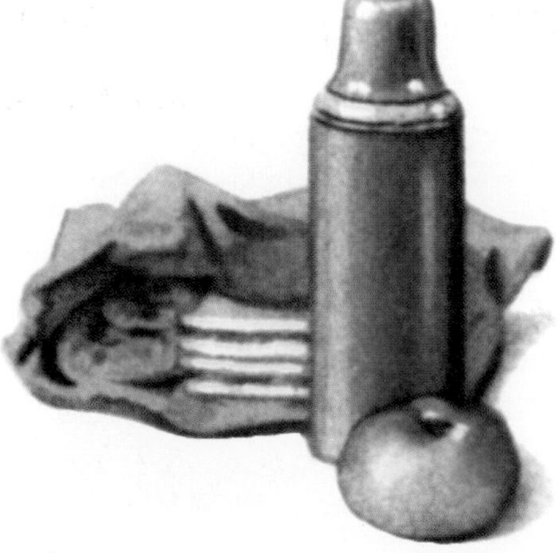

lunch غَدَاء

gha-daa'

lynx وَشَق

wa-shaq

magazine مَجَلَّة

ma-jal-la

magician ساحِر

saa-Hir

magnet مَغْنَطِيس

magh-na-Tees

map خَرِيطَة

kha-ree-Ta

maple leaf وَرْقَةُ القَيْقَب

wa-ra-qa-tul qay-qab

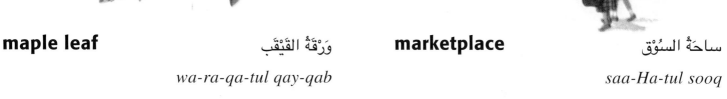

marketplace ساحَةُ السُوْق

saa-Ha-tul sooq

mask قِنَاع

qi-naa‘

messy غَيْر مُرَتَّب *ghair mu-rat-tab*

milkman بائِعُ الحَلِيب *baa-ee-'ul Haleeb*

mirror مِرْآة *mir-aat*

mitten كَفٌّ بِلا أَصابِع *kaf-fun bi-laa a-Saa-bi'*

money نُقُود *nu-qood*

monkey قِرْد *qird*

moon قَمَر *qa-mar*

mother أُم

umm

mountain جَبَل

ja-bal

mouse فَأْر

fa'r

mouth فَم

fam

mushroom فُطْر

fu-Tr

music مُوسِيقَى

moo-see-qa

naked عُرْيان *'ur-yaan*

necklace عِقْد *'iqd*

needle إِبْرَة *ib-ra*

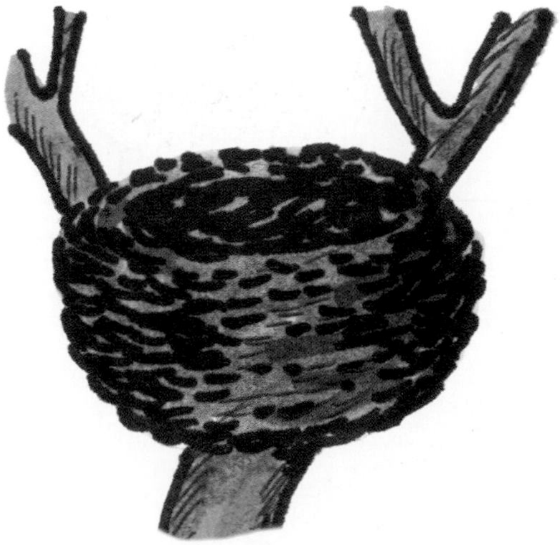

nest عُشّ *'ush*

newspaper جَرِيدَة *ja-ree-da*

nightingale بُلْبُل

bul-bul

nine تِسْعَة

tis-'a

notebook دَفْتَر

daf-tar

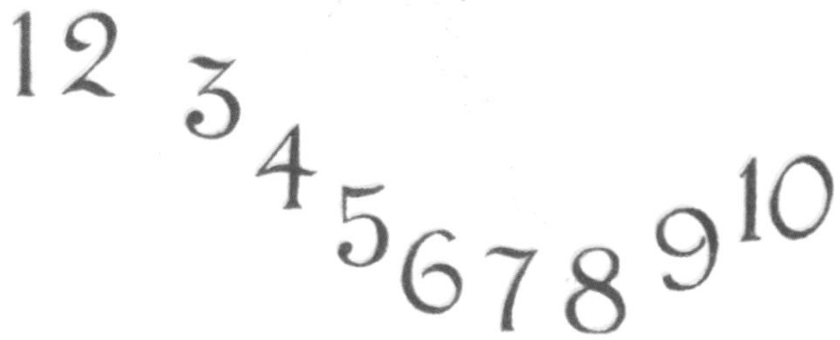

number عَدَد

'a-dad

nut جَوْز

jawz

oar مِجْذاف
mij-dhaaf

ocean liner سَفِينَة
sa-fee-na

old عَجُوز
'a-jooz

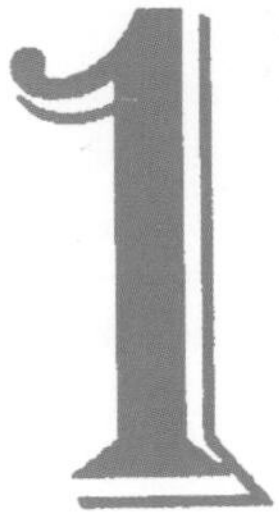

one واحِد
waa-Hid

onion بَصَل
ba-Sal

open مَفْتُوح

maf-TooH

orange بُرْتُقَال

bur-tu-qaal

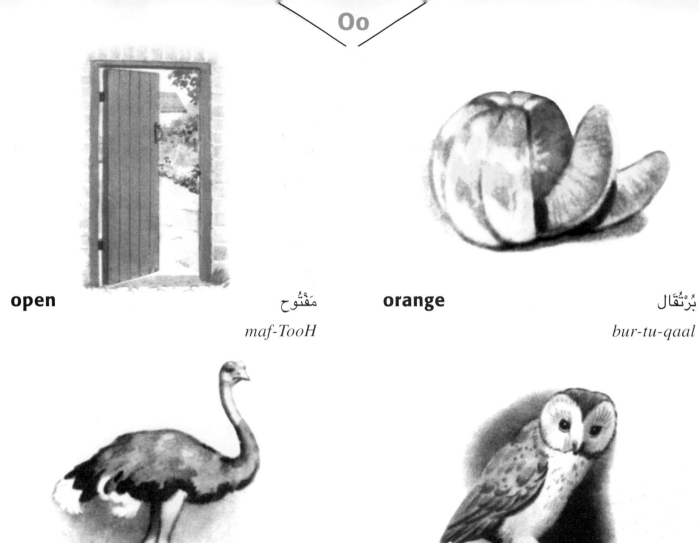

ostrich نَعَامَة

na-'aa-ma

owl بُوْمَة

boo-ma

ox ثَوْر

thawr

padlock قُفْل

qufl

paint دِهَان

di-haan

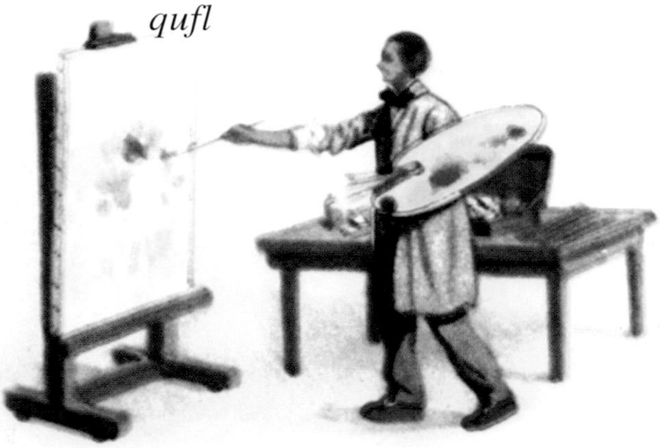

painter رَسَّام

ras-saam

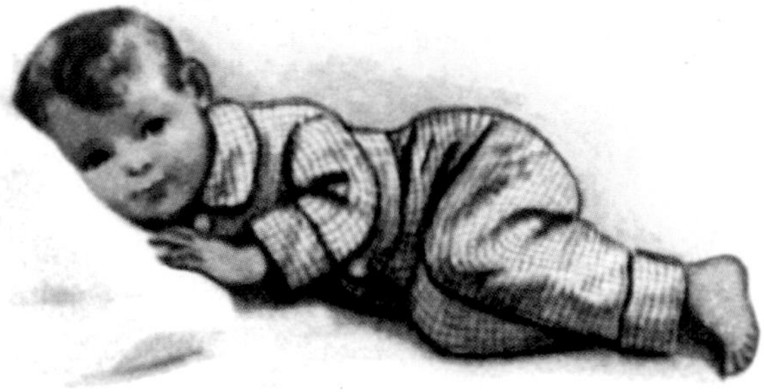

pajamas بِيجَامَة

bee-jaa-ma

palm tree نَخْلَة

nakh-la

paper وَرَقَة

wa-ra-qa

parachute مِظَلَّةُ هُبُوط

mi-Zal-latu hu-booT

park مُنْتَزَه

mun-ta-zah

parrot بَبَّغَاء

ba-ba-ghaa'

passport جَوَازُ سَفَر

ja-waa-zu sa-far

patch رُقْعَة

ruq-'a

path مَمَرّ

ma-marr

peach خَوْخ/دُرَّاق

khawkh/dur-raaq

pear كُمَّثْرَى/إِجَّاص

kum-math-ra/eej-jaas

pebble حَصَاة

Ha-Saat

(to) peck نَقَرَ

na-qa-ra

(to) peel قَشَّرَ

qa-sha-ra

pelican بَجَع

ba-ja‘

pencil قَلَم

qa-lam

penguin بِطْرِيق

biT-reeq

people ناس

naas

piano بِيَانُو

bi-yaa-noo

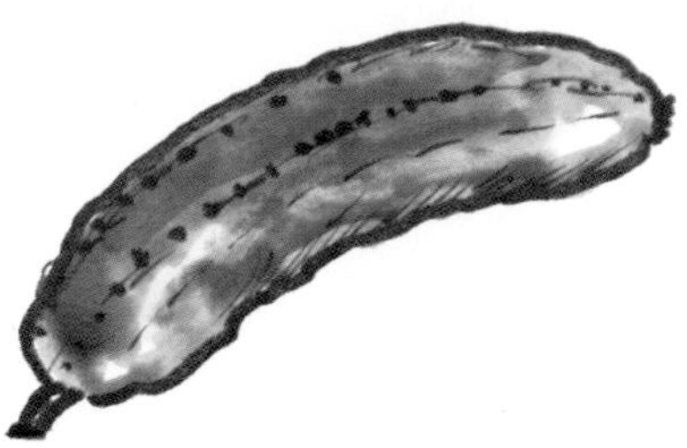

pickle مُخَلَّل

mu-khal-lal

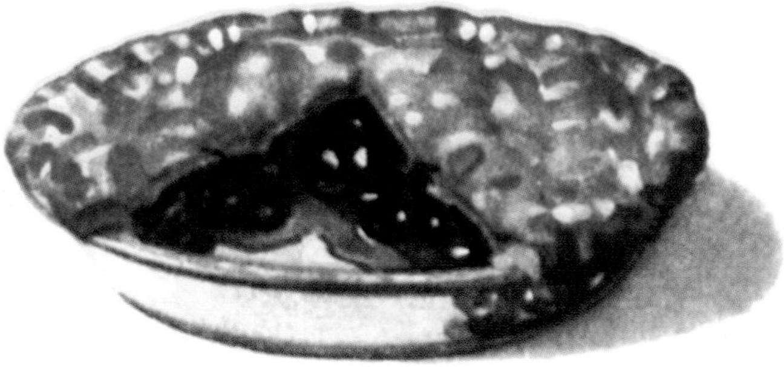

pie فَطِيرَة

fa-Tee-ra

pig خِنْزِير

khin-zeer

pigeon حَمَام

Ha-maam

pillow وِسَادَة

wi-saa-da

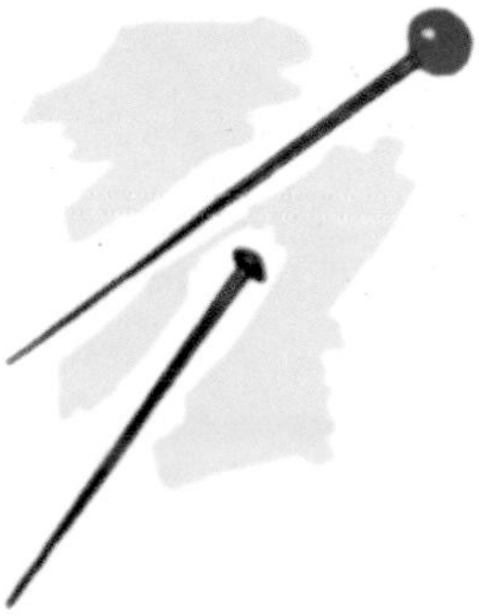

pin دَبُّوس

dab-boos

pine صَنَوْبَر

Sa-naw-bar

pineapple أَنَانَاس

a-naa-naas

pit نَوَاة

na-waat

pitcher إِبْرِيق

ib-reeq

plate صَحْن

SaHn

platypus مِنْقَارُ البَطَّة

min-qaa-rul baT-Ta

(to) play

لَعَبَ

la-'a-ba

plum

بُرْقُوق/خَوْخ

bur-qooq/khawkh

polar bear

دُبٌّ قُطْبِيّ

dub-bun quT-biy

pony

فَرَسٌ قَزَم

fa-ra-sun qa-zam

pot

حَلَّة/طَنْجَرَة

Hal-la/Tan-ja-ra

potato

بَطَاطِس/بَطَاطَا

ba-Taa-Tis/ba-Taa-Ta

(to) pour سَكَبَ

sa-ka-ba

present هَدِيَّة

ha-diy-ya

(to) pull شَدَّ

shad-da

pumpkin قَرْع

qar'

Qq

puppy جَرْو

ja-roo

queen مَلِكَة

ma-li-ka

rabbit

أَرْنَب

ar-nab

raccoon

راكُون

raa-koon

racket

مِضْرَب

miD-rab

radio

رادْيُو

raad-yo

radish

فُجْل

fujl

raft رَمَث

ra-math

rain مَطَر

ma-Tar

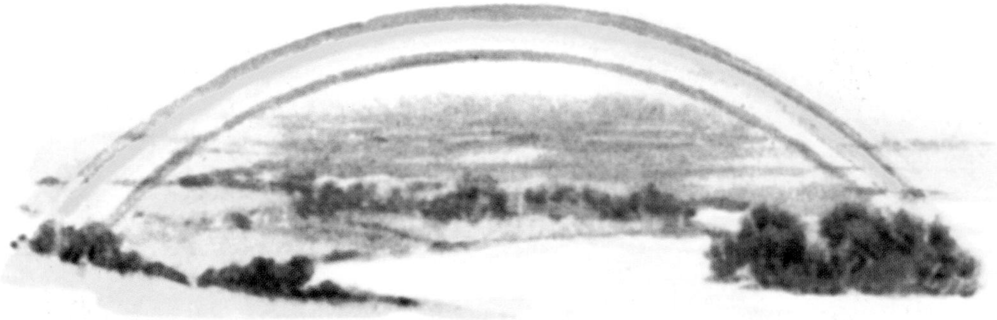

rainbow قَوْسُ قُزَح

qaw-su qu-zaH

raincoat مِعْطَفُ ضِدّ المَطَر

mi'-Ta-fun Didd al-ma-Tar

raspberry تُوْتُ شَوْكِيّ

too-tun shaw-kiy

(to) read قَرَأَ

qa-ra-'a

red أَحْمَر

aHmar

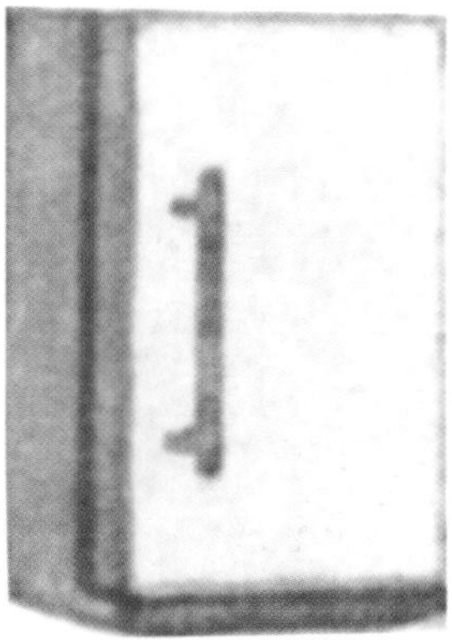

refrigerator ثَلاَّجَة

thal-laa-ja

rhinoceros كَرْكَدَنّ

kar-ka-dann

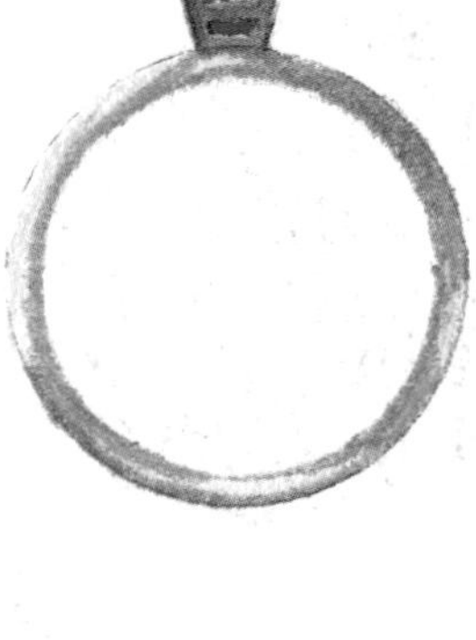

ring خاتِم

khaa-tim

(to) ring دَقَّ الجَرَس

daq-qal ja-ras

river نَهْر

nahr

road طَرِيق

Ta-reeq

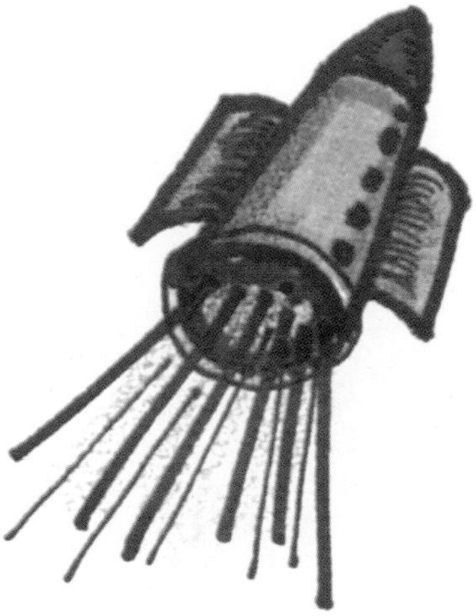

rocket صارُوخ

Saa-rookh

roof سَطْحُ البَيْت

saT-Hul bayt

rooster دِيك

deek

root جِذْر
ji-dhr

rope حَبْل
Habl

rose وَرْدَة
war-da

(to) row جَذَفَ
ja-dha-fa

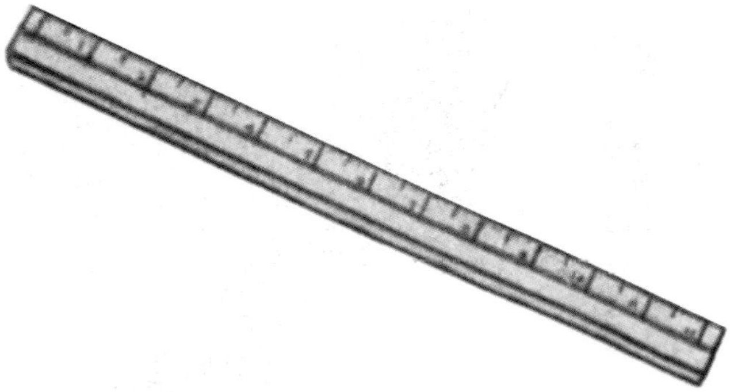

ruler مِسْطَرَة
mis-Ta-ra

(to) run رَكَضَ
ra-ka-Da

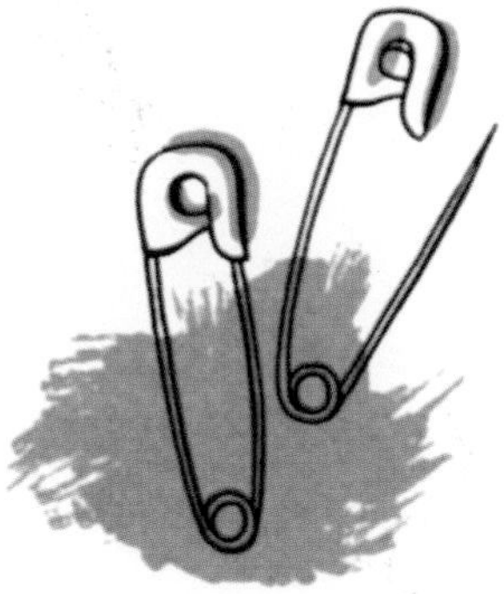

safety pin دَبُّوسُ الأَمَان

dab-boo-sul a-maan

(to) sail أَبْحَرَ

ab-Ha-ra

sailor بَحَّار

baH-Haar

salt مِلْح

milH

scarf وِشَاح

wi-shaaH

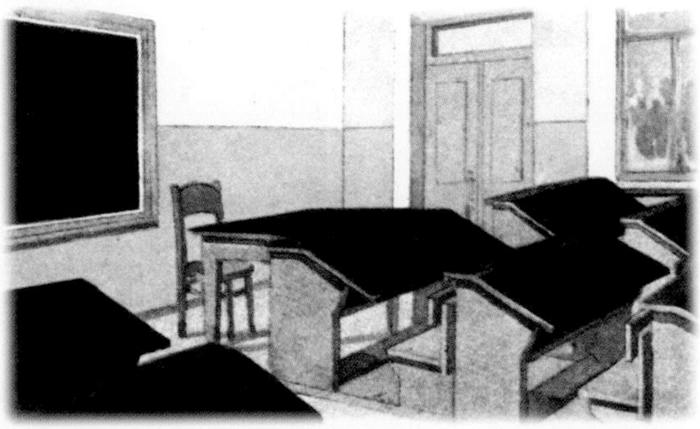

school مَدْرَسَة

mad-ra-sa

scissors مِقَصّ

mi-qaSS

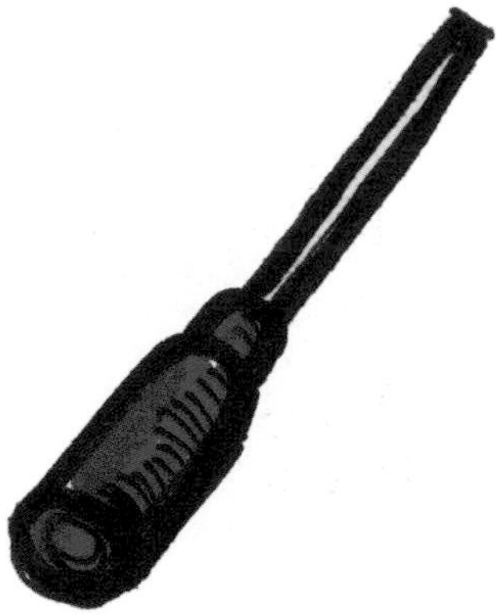

screwdriver مِفَكّ

mi-fakk

seagull نَوْرَس

naw-ras

seesaw نَوَّاسَة

naw-waa-sa

seven سَبْعَة

sab-'a

(to) sew خَيَّطَ

khay-ya-Ta

shark قِرْش
qirsh

sheep خَرُوف
kha-roof

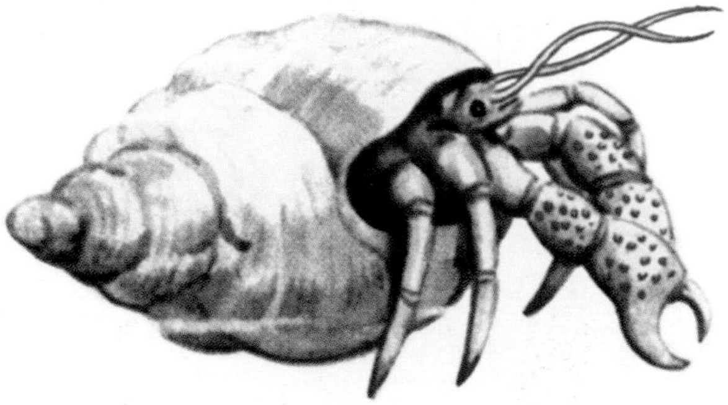

shell صَدَفَة
Sa-da-fa

shepherd راعٍ
raa-'een

ship باخِرَة
baa-khi-ra

shirt قَمِيص
qa-meeS

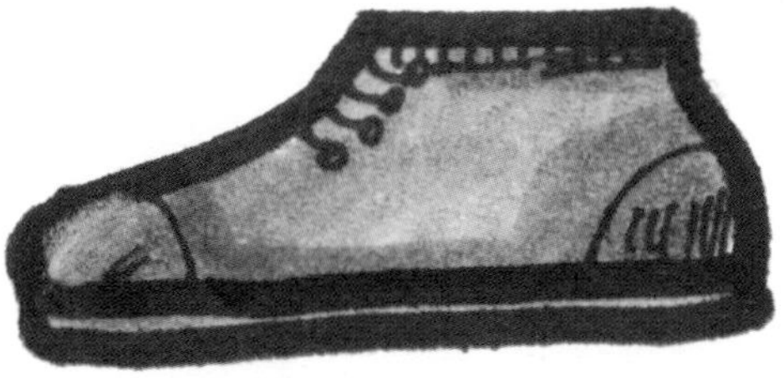

shoe جَزْمَة/حِذَاء

jaz-ma/Hi-dhaa'

shovel مِجْرَفَة

mij-ra-fa

(to) show عَرَضَ

'a-ra-Da

shower دُشّ

dush

shutter شِيْش

sheesh

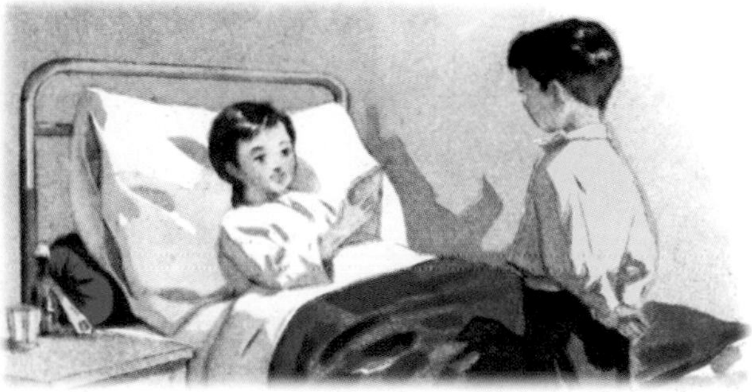

sick مَرِيض

ma-reeD

sieve مُنْخُل

mun-khul

(to) sing غَنَّى

ghan-na

(to) sit جَلَسَ

ja-la-sa

six سِتَّة

sit-ta

sled مِزْلَقَة

miz-la-qa

(to) sleep نامَ

naa-ma

small صَغِير

Sa-gheer

smile اِبْتِسَامَة

ib-ti-saa-ma

snail حَلَزُون

Ha-la-zoon

snake حَيَّة

Hay-ya

snow ثَلْج

thalj

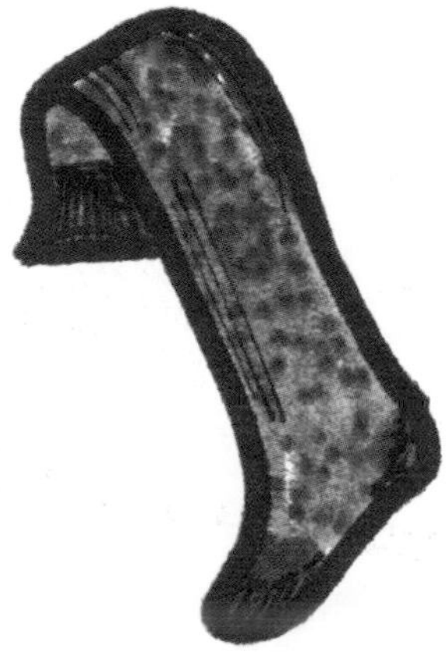

sock جَوَارِب/كَلْسات

ja-waa-rib/kal-saat

sofa أَرِيكَة

a-ree-ka

sparrow عُصْفُور

'uS-foor

spider عَنْكَبُوت

'an-ka-boot

spiderweb بَيْتُ العَنْكَبُوت

bay-tul 'an-ka-boot

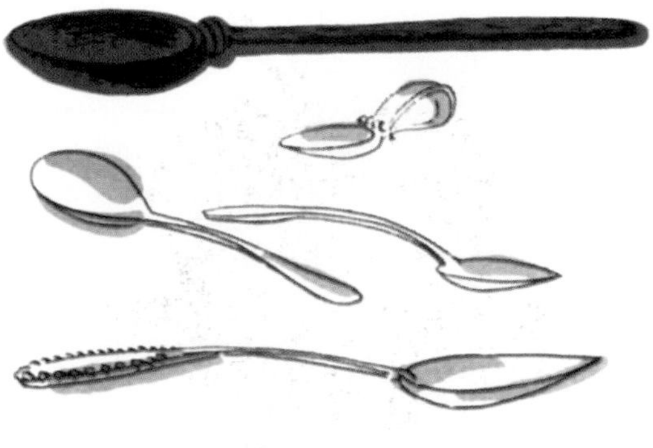

spoon مِلْعَقَة

mil-'a-qa

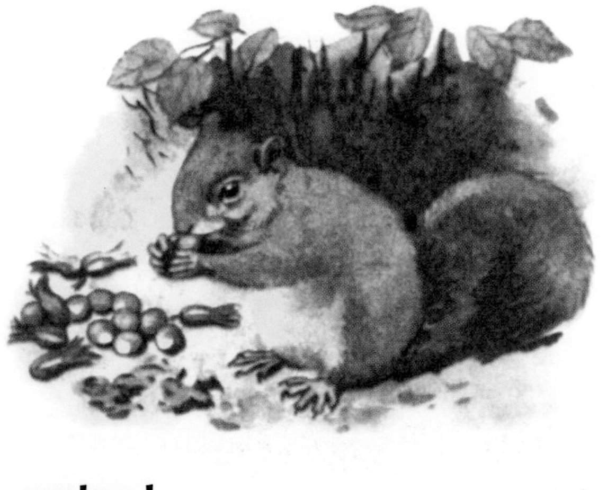

squirrel سِنْجاب

sin-jaab

stairs دَرَج
dar-raj

stamp طابَعُ بَرِيدِيّ
Taa-ba-'un ba-ree-diy

starfish نَجْمُ البَحْر
naj-mul baHr

stork لَقْلَق
laq-laq

stove مَوْقِد
maw-qid

strawberry فَرَاوْلَة/فِريز
fa-raaw-la/fraiz

subway

مِتْرُو نَفَقِيّ

mi-troo na-fa-qiy

sugar cube

مُكَعَّبُ سُكَّر

mu-qa'-'abu suk-kar

sun

شَمْس

shams

sunflower

عَبَّادُ الشَّمْس

'ab-baa-dul shams

sweater

سِتْرَة

sit-ra

(to) sweep

كَنَسَ

ka-na-sa

swing

أُرْجُوحَة

ur-ju-Ha

table مائِدَة

ma-'i-da

teapot إِبْرِيقُ الشَّاي

ib-ree-qul shaay

teddy bear دُبٌّ قُمَاشِيّ

dub-bun qu-maa-shiy

television تِلِفِزْيُون

ti-li-fiz-yoon

ten عَشَرَة

'a-sha-ra

tent خَيْمَة

khay-ma

theater مَسْرَح
maS-raH

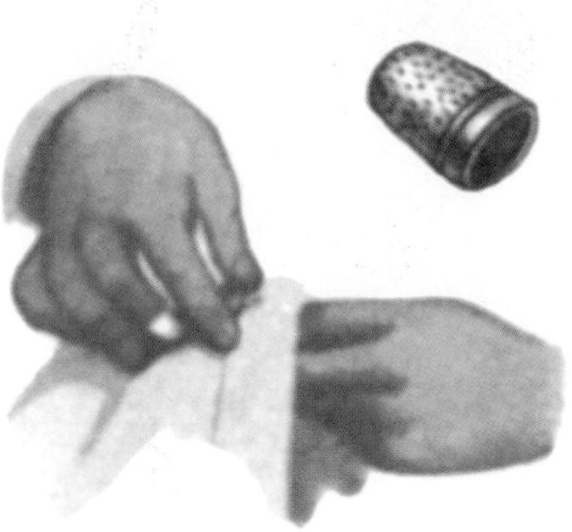

thimble كُشْتُبَان
kush-tu-baan

(to) think فَكَّرَ
fak-ka-ra

three ثَلاَثَة
tha-laa-tha

tie كَرافات
kraa-faat

(to) tie رَبَطَ
ra-ba-Ta

tiger نِمْر

nimr

toaster مِحْمَصَةُ خُبْزٍ كَهْرَبائِيَّة

miH-ma-Sa-tu khub-zin kah-ra-baa-iy-ya

tomato طَمَاطِم/بَنَدُورَة

Ta-maa-tim/ba-na-doo-ra

toucan طُوقان

too-qaan

towel فُوْطَة

foo-Ta

tower بُرْج

burj

toy box عُلْبَةُ اللُعَب

'ul-ba-tul lu-'ab

tracks خُطُوطُ السِّكَّة الحَدِيدِيَّة

khu-Too-tul sik-kal Ha-dee-diy-ya

train station مَحَطَّةُ القِطَار

ma-HaT-Ta-tul qi-Taar

tray صِيْنِيَّة

See-niy-ya

tree شَجَرَة

sha-ja-ra

trough مِعْلَف

mi'-laf

truck شاحِنَة *shaa-Hi-na*

trumpet بُوْق *booq*

tulip تُولِيب *tu-leep*

tunnel نَفَق *na-faq*

turtle سُلَحْفاة *su-laH-faat*

twins تَوْأَمان *taw-'a-maan*

two إِثْنان *ith-naan*

umbrella مِظَلَّة
mi-Zal-la

uphill مُرْتَقَى
mur-ta-qa

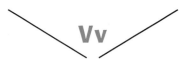

Vv

vase زَهْرِيَّة
zah-riy-ya

veil حِجَاب
Hi-jaab

village قَرْيَة

qar-ya

violet بَنَفْسَج

ba-naf-saj

violin كَمَان

ka-maan

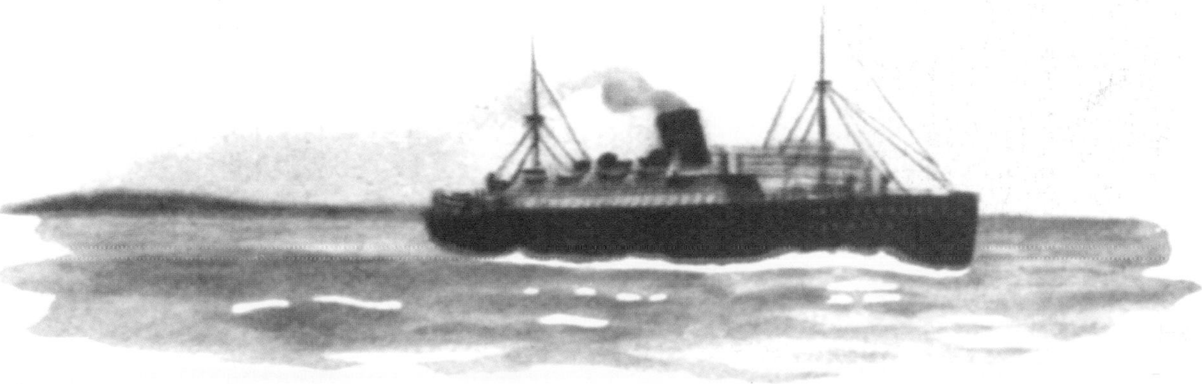

voyage رِحْلَة

riH-la

waiter سُفْرَجِي

suf-ra-ji

(to) wake up اِسْتَيْقَظَ

is-tay-qa-Za

walrus فَظ

faZ

(to) wash غَسَلَ

gha-sa-la

watch ساعَة

saa-'a

(to) watch راقَبَ

raa-qa-ba

(to) water سَقَى

sa-qa

waterfall شَلاَّل

sha-laal

watering can مِرَشَّة

mi-rash-sha

watermelon بِطِّيخ

biT-Teekh

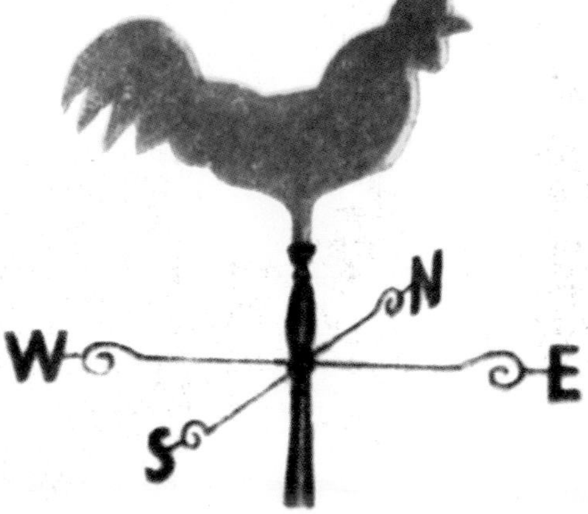

weather vane دَوَّارَةُ الهَوَاء

daw-waa-ra-tul ha-waa'

(to) weigh وَزَنَ

wa-za-na

whale حُوْت

Hoot

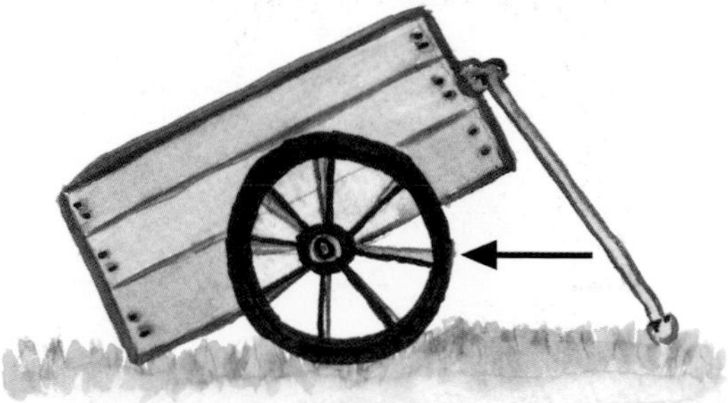

wheel عَجَلَة

'a-ja-la

wheelbarrow عَرَبَةُ يَد

'a-ra-ba-tu yad

whiskers شارِبُ الحَيَوَان

shaa-ri-bul Ha-ya-waan

(to) whisper هَمَسَ

ha-ma-sa

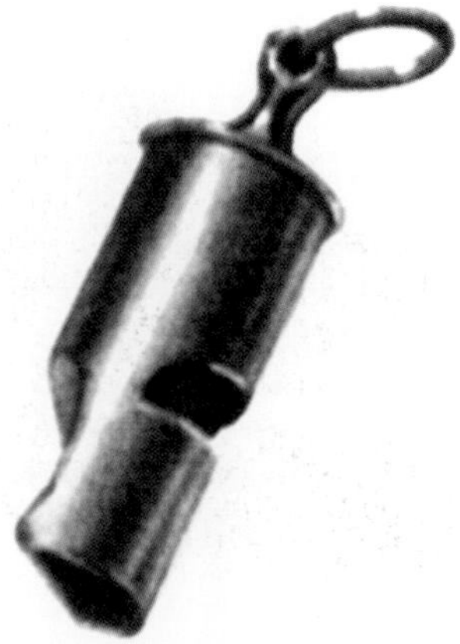

whistle صَفَّارَة

Saf-faa-ra

white أَبْيَض

ab-yaD

wig شَعْرٌ مُسْتَعار

sha'-run mus-ta-'aar

wind رِيح

reeH

window شُبَّاك

shub-baak

wings أَجْنِحَة

aj-ni-Ha

winter شِتَاء

shi-taa'

wolf ذِئْب

dhi-'b

wood خَشَب

kha-shab

word كَلِمَة

ka-li-ma

(to) write كَتَبَ

ka-ta-ba

yellow

أَصْفَر

aS-far

Zz

zebra

حِمَارٌ وَحْشِيّ

Hi-maa-run waH-shiy

أ

أَب	father
اِبْتِسَامَة	smile
أَبْجَدِيَّة	alphabet
أَبْحَرَ	(to) sail
إِبْرَة	needle
إِبْرِيق	pitcher
إِبْرِيقُ الشَّاي	teapot
أَبْيَض	white
أَثَاث	furniture
إِثْنَان	two
إِجَّاص	pear
أَجْنِحَة	wings
اِحْتَضَنَ	(to) hug
أُحْجِيَةُ الصُّوَر المَقْطُوعَة	jigsaw puzzle
أَحْمَر	red
أَخ	brother
اِخْتَبَأَ	(to) hide
أَخْضَر	green
أَرْبَعَة	four
أُرْجُوحَة	swing
أُرْجُوحَةٌ شَبَكِيَّة	hammock
أَرْنَب	rabbit
أَرِيكَة	sofa
أَزْرَق	blue
اِسْتَكْشَفَ	(to) explore
اِسْتَمَعَ	(to) listen
اِسْتَيْقَظَ	(to) wake up
أَسَد	lion
أَسْكِيمو	Eskimo
أَسْمَر	brown
أَسْوَد	black
إِصْبَع	finger
اِصْطَادَ	(to) fish
أَصْفَر	yellow
أَعْطَى	(to) give
أَكَلَ	(to) eat
آلَةٌ مُوسِيقِيَّة	instrument
أُم	mother
أَمْتِعَة	luggage
أَنَانَاس	pineapple
أَيِّل	deer

ب

بائِعُ الحَلِيب	milkman
باخِرَة	ship
باذِنْجان	eggplant
بالُون	balloon
بَبَّغاء	parrot
البَبَّغَاءُ المُتَيَّمَة	lovebird
بَجَع	pelican
بَحَّار	sailor
بُرْتُقال	orange
بُرْج	tower
بُرْقُوق	plum
بِرْمِيل	barrel
بِرْواز	frame
بَسْكَوِيت	cracker
بَصَل	onion
بَطّ	duck
بَطَاطِس/بَطاطا	potato
بِطْرِيق	penguin
بِطِّيخ	watermelon
بَقَرَة	cow
بَكَى	(to) cry
بُلْبُل	nightingale
بِنْت	girl
بَنَدُورَة	tomato
بَنَفْسَج	violet
بَنْك	bench
بَهْلَوَان	juggler
بَوَّابَة	gate
بُوْصُلَة	compass
بُوظَة	ice cream
بُوق	trumpet
بُومَة	owl
بُونْبُون	candy
بِيَانُو	piano
بَيْت	house
بَيْتٌ زُجَاجِيّ	greenhouse
بَيْتُ العَرُوسَة	dollhouse
بَيْتُ العَنْكَبُوت	spiderweb
بِيجَامَة	pajamas
بَيْض	egg

ت

تاج	crown
تاريخ	date
تاكْسِي	cab
تِبْن	hay
تَزَلُّج عَلَى الجَلِيد	ice-skating
تِسْعَة	nine
تَسَلَّقَ	(to) climb
تُفَّاحَة	apple
تلفزْيُون	television
تِنِّين	dragon

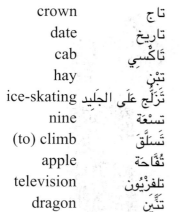

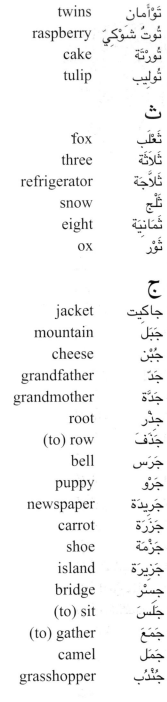

مِجْذاف	oar
مَجَلَّة	magazine
مِحَش	lawn mower
مَحَطَّةُ القِطار	train station
مِحْمَصَةُ خُبْزٍ كَهْرَبائِيَّة	toaster
مُخَلَّل	pickle
مِدْخَنَة	chimney
مَدْرَسَة	school
مِرْآة	mirror
مُرَبَّى	jam
مُرْتَقى	uphill
مِرَشَّة	watering can
مِرْوَحَة	fan
مَرِيض	sick
مِزْلَقَة	sled
مَسْرَح	theater
مِشْط	comb
مِصْباحُ جَيْب	flashlight
مِضَخَّةُ الحَرِيق	hydrant
مِضْرَب	racket
مَطَر	rain
مِطْرَقَة	hammer
مِظَلَّة	umbrella
مِظَلَّةُ هُبُوط	parachute
مَعَ السَلامَة	"Good-bye"
مِعْزَى	goat
مِعْطَف	coat
مِعْطَفُ ضِد المَطَر	raincoat
مِعْلَف	trough
مِسْطَرَة	ruler
مَغْنَطِيس	magnet
مِصْباح	lamp
مِفْتاح	key
مَفْتُوح	open
مِفَك	screwdriver
مِقَصّ	scissors
مَقْهَى	café
مَكْتَب	desk
مُكَعَّبُ سُكَّر	sugar cube
مُكَعَّباتُ ثَلْج	ice cubes
مِكْنَسَة	broom
مِكْواة	iron
مُلَبَّس	candy
مِلْح	salt
مِلْعَقَة	spoon
مَلْفُوف	cabbage
مَلِكَة	queen
مَمَرّ	path
مَنارَة	lighthouse
مُنْتَزَه	park
مُنْخُل	sieve
مِنْديل	handkerchief
مِنْظار	binoculars
مِنْقارُ البَطَّة	platypus
مَهْد	cradle
مُهَرِّج	clown
مَوْزَة	banana
مُوسِيقَى	music
مَوْقِد	stove

ن

نار	fire
ناس	people
نافُورَة	fountain
نامَ	sleep
نَجْمُ البَحْر	starfish
نَحْلَة	bee
نَحْلَةٌ كَبِيرَة طَنَّانَة	bumblebee
نَخْلَة	palm tree
نَسْر	eagle
نَظَّارَة	glasses
نَعامَة	ostrich
نَفَق	tunnel
نَقَرَ	(to) peck
نُقُود	money
نَمِر	tiger
نَهْر	river
نَواة	pit
نَوَّاسَة	seesaw
نَوْر	blossom
نَوْرَس	seagull

هـ

هَدِيَّة	present
هَمَسَ	whisper
هَمْسْتَر	hamster

و

واحِد	one
وَجْه	face
وَرْدَة	rose
وَرَقُ اللَّعِب	card
وَرَقَة	leaf; paper
وَرَقَةُ القَيْقَب	maple leaf
وَزَّة	goose
وَزَنَ	(to) weight
وِسادَة	pillow
وِشاح	scarf
وَشَق	lynx
وَلَد	boy

ي

يَد	hand

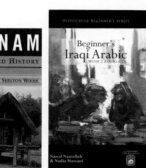

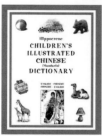

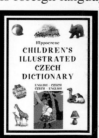

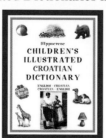

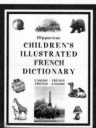

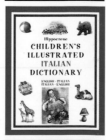

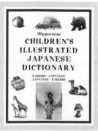

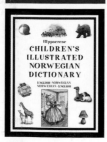

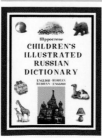

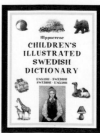